4P GROWTH FRAMEWORK

Guaranteed Science for 3x Consistent Growth in TMT Dealership

4P GROWTH FRAMEWORK

Guaranteed Science for
3x Consistent Growth in
TMT Dealership

GOPAL RATHI   DHRUV RATHI

Worldwide Published by
Pendown Press

PENDOWN PRESS LLP
An ISO 9001 & ISO 14001 Certified Co.
Regd. Office 3767A, Kanhaiya Nagar,
Tri Nagar, Delhi-110035
Ph.: 8180886000, 9650072927, 8595249536
E-mail: info@pendownpress.com
Branch Office 1A/2A, 20, Hari Sadan, Ansari Road,
Daryaganj, New Delhi-110002
Ph.: 011-45794768
Website: PendownPress.com

First Edition: 2023

ISBN: 978-93-5554-639-5

All Rights Reserved
All the ideas and thoughts in this book are given by the author and he is responsible for the treatise, facts and dialogues used in this book. He is also responsible for the used pictures and the permission to use them in this book. Copyright of this book is reserved with the author. The publisher does not have any responsibility for the above-mentioned matters. No part of this publication may be reproduced, distributed, or transmitted in any form or by any means, including photocopying, recording, or other electronic or mechanical methods, without the prior written permission of the publisher and author.

Layout and Cover Designed by Pendown Graphics Team
Printed and Bound in India by Thomson ress India Ltd.

Dedication

We lovingly dedicate this book
to our parents, Mr Anil Rathi
and Mrs Urmil Rathi.
Without their unconditional love,
support and sacrifices, we would have
never accomplished what we have been
able to. They continue to be our endless
source of inspiration & action.

Contents

Preface

Are you a TMT Bar Dealer? Or an aspiring TMT Bar Dealer? Or perhaps just someone on the lookout for a great business opportunity?

If you answer yes to any of the above and are eager to become a super-successful entrepreneur in the TMT Bar ecosystem, creating personal prosperity while contributing to the development & economic growth of the nation, then please keep reading.

Whether you are an existing seasoned dealer, an existing new dealer or just wanting to start out- This book is your guide & blueprint to running a successful TMT Bar Dealership.

The TMT Bar market is vast and brimming with potential. However, with great opportunity come significant challenges. The competition is intense and has degenerated to the level of price wars instead of being focused on quality, benefits and customer service.

However, with the right choice of partnership, support and strategies, anyone can build and sustain a successful and profitable TMT Bar Dealership.

This book is designed to provide you with practical advice & actionable steps condensed into the well-researched.

"4P Growth Framework"–

"Guaranteed Science for 3x Consistent Growth in TMT Dealership."

This book not only gives you the framework but goes a step further and shows you how to apply it to overcome real-life challenges that all TMT Bar Dealerships commonly face.

By the end of this book, you will be able to use the Framework to overcome any and all challenges that crop up even on a day-to-day basis and keep growing consistently.

Thank you for choosing this book; it shows how committed you are to your growth. We assure you that this book will be well worth the precious time you invest in it.

Let's begin the journey to growth and profitability...

Acknowledgements

Writing this book has been a challenging yet immensely fulfilling journey. This journey was made smoother and easier by many people. We are immensely grateful to every one who contributed directly or indirectly to the fruition of this book.

First and foremost a special mention to our family for their unconditional support and for allowing us to take some time that belonged to them in bringing this project to completion.

Our heartfelt gratitude to our mentor, Mr Akshar Yadav for his guidance and motivation on this project and always.

A huge bouquet of thanks to our business coach Mr Rahul Jain for making us strive for and achieve inclusive excellence.

A big shoutout to friends of the GO Community for their help and guidance. It's a great feeling to know that this wonderful community is cheering us on.

Special & sincere thanks to our dealers and distributors for giving us a very detailed insight into the workings of a TMT Bar Dealership.

Finally, we'd like to thank Mr Dinesh Verma, CEO, Pendown Press & his capable team for supporting and guiding us during the course of writing this book from start to finish.

Mapping & Mining the Vast Market Potential of TMT Bars

The demand for TMT bars in India is currently witnessing a significant surge.

India's high growth imperative in 2023 and beyond will significantly be driven by major strides in key sectors, with infrastructure development being a critical force aiding the progress. Infrastructure will play a key role in helping India become a US$ 26 trillion economy. The sector is highly responsible for propelling India's overall development and enjoys intense focus from the Government for initiating policies that would ensure the time-bound creation of world-class infrastructure in the country.

Prime Minister Narendra Modi also recently reiterated that infrastructure is a crucial pillar to ensure good governance across sectors.

The government's focus on building the infrastructure of the future is evident from the many initiatives launched recently. The US$ 1.3 trillion national master plan for infrastructure, Gati Shakti, is the forerunner and has already shown significant headway.

Infrastructure support to the nation's manufacturers also remains one of the top agendas as it will significantly transform goods and exports movement making freight delivery effective and economical.

The "Smart Cities Mission" and "Housing for All" programs are all potentials for the infrastructure and building industry have benefited from these initiatives. Saudi Arabia seeks to spend up to US$ 100 billion in India in energy, petrochemicals, refinery, infrastructure, agriculture, minerals, and mining.

The infrastructure sector includes power, bridges, dams, roads, and urban infrastructure development. In other words, the infrastructure sector acts as a catalyst for India's economic growth as it drives the growth of related sectors like townships, housing, built-up infrastructure and construction development projects.

In order to meet India's aim of reaching a US$ 5 trillion economy by 2025, infrastructure development is the need of the hour. The government has launched the National Infrastructure Pipeline (NIP) combined with other initiatives such as 'Make in India' and the production-linked incentives (PLI) scheme to augment the growth of the infrastructure sector.

"Under Budget 2023-24, capital investment outlay for infrastructure is being increased by 33% to Rs. 10 lakh crore (US$ 122 billion), which would be 3.3% of GDP and almost three times the outlay in 2019-20." - India Brand Equity Foundation, An Initiative of the Ministry of Commerce and Industry, GOI.

With the Covid-19 pandemic fully over now, the following 20 Indian Megaprojects & Technologies are Set to Transform Our Country-

Bullet Train	Solar Mission by ISRO
Hyperloop project in India	Mumbai Trans Harbor link
Gaganyaan	Setu Bharatam
World's first motorable road through Glaciers	Kalpasar Project
World's highest rail bridge: Chenab bridge	Bharatmala Project
Char Dham expressway	Indian Rivers Inter-link Project
Char Dham railway	Zanskar highway
Mumbai Delhi expressway	Electric vehicle industry in India
New metro lines across cities	Launch of 5G in India
Sagar Mala project	Indian regional navigation satellite system

With the country's robust infrastructure development and construction activities, the construction industry's demand for TMT bars has skyrocketed.

The government's focus on initiatives like "Housing for All" and the development of "Smart Cities" has further fuelled this demand. Additionally, the increasing urbanization and growing population have led to a rise in residential and commercial construction projects nationwide.

As a result, steel manufacturers are experiencing a surge in orders for TMT bars, prompting them to increase production capacities to meet the ever-growing demand. The trend indicates a promising future for the TMT bar industry in India.

The current scenario of the supply of TMT bars in India is characterized by a mixed bag of factors. While the demand for TMT bars is on the rise, the industry has been grappling with some challenges in the supply chain. The fluctuations in the availability of raw materials, such as iron ore and coal, have impacted the production of TMT bars. Additionally, logistical issues and transportation constraints have further strained the supply chain, causing delays in deliveries.

However, steel manufacturers are working towards expanding their production capacities and streamlining their supply chains to meet the growing demand. Efforts are being made to ensure a steady and sufficient supply of TMT bars to support the construction industry's needs.

The growth potential of this industry appears unlimited, and the future is extremely profitable and prosperous for those who deliver on time quality using ethical business practices while learning to ride technology.

Current Scenario in the TMT Dealerships

The current scenario of TMT retail shops in India is witnessing a vibrant and competitive landscape. With the surge in construction activities and infrastructure development projects, the demand for TMT bars has soared.

This has led to an increase in the number of retail shops specializing in TMT bars across the country. These retail shops cater to a wide range of customers, including individual homeowners, contractors, and builders. They offer various brands and grades of TMT bars, providing customers with a wide selection to choose from. Moreover, many retail shops are also embracing digital platforms, allowing customers to explore and purchase TMT bars online.

The competitive market ensures that customers have access to competitive prices and excellent customer service from these retail outlets.

The main reason for the expected growth of TMT bar dealers in India over the next few years can be attributed to the booming construction and infrastructure sectors in the country. India is experiencing rapid urbanization and industrialization, leading to increased demand for residential and commercial spaces, as well as infrastructure development such as roads, bridges, and power plants.

TMT bars, known for their superior strength and durability, are essential construction materials. As a result, TMT bar dealers are poised to benefit from this growth trajectory.

Navigating the Threats

While the market potential is vast, the main threat to TMT bar dealers in India is the intense competition within the market.

With the construction industry experiencing significant growth, numerous TMT bar manufacturers and dealers have emerged, leading to a highly competitive landscape. This competition puts pressure on dealers to differentiate themselves and offer unique value propositions to attract customers. Additionally, fluctuations in raw material prices can impact the profitability of TMT bar dealers. Economic factors such as inflation, currency fluctuations, and government policies also pose risks to the industry.

It is essential for TMT bar dealers to adapt to changing market dynamics, maintain quality standards, and focus on customer satisfaction to stay ahead in this competitive environment.

So, if you are a part of this growing & increasingly lucrative industry---

Congratulations! You are in the right place at the right time!

However, the million-rupee question is this: ARE YOU DOING THE RIGHT THING?

Having a combined experience of more than 60 years, we have met 1000s of dealers and understood their journey as

TMT dealers. Among the journeys we witnessed were the journey of a 50-year-old dealer of our brand and also of a 7-day-old dealer of our brand.

Surprisingly, the situations being faced by them were more or less similar.

These situations, if not handled properly, will stop the growth of their business or lead to nominal year-on-year growth.

Apart from lower growth, the dealership can also face challenges like money getting stuck in the market, the new generation not being interested in joining the dealership, blacklisting of the dealership by customers etc.

In the next section of the book, we will share with you our 4P Growth Framework for 3X Consistent growth of your dealership, along with some common Real Life Situations that threaten the growth of TMT Dealerships today and how using the 4P Framework you can overcome these challenges smoothly and speedily.

This will enable your dealership to have extraordinary and peaceful business growth. Apart from growth, you can also achieve the following milestones using this framework to overcome these commonly faced situations successfully-

1. Achieving the fastest repeat business with minimum involvement.

2. Expanding to multiple outlets.

3. A Peaceful night's sleep (every single night).

4. A proud presence in the market.

5. A systemized, process-driven approach.

6. A better business experience.

But before we go any further, we would like you to participate in this exercise and make a list of situations which are not letting you achieve your desired growth. Once you are finished with the book, you will know exactly which 'P' from the framework to apply and overcome the challenge.

____

____

____

____

____

____

____

____

____

Oh! I think I just heard you asking the question, "So exactly who are we to be teaching you all this with such confidence and guarantee?"

Sincere apologies for not introducing ourselves yet. We are Gopal & Dhruv Rathi, proudly carrying forward the legacy of the Rathi Group--- India's First & Oldest name in the TMT Bar Industry as Directors of the Shri Rathi Group.

Though our group's 80 years of service to the nation are known to almost everyone within & outside the industry, let us take you on the inspiring journey of the history & legacy of our group, and you will understand why we speak with such in-depth knowledge and confidence.

80 Glorious Years of the Rathi Group Serving the Nation!

How the Legacy Began...

The prosperous empire impacting the entire nation that we see today as Rathi Steel Group has its roots in a small village called Maroth in Rajasthan (then) but is today a part of Pakistan. The Rathi family migrated to Delhi somewhere in the 18th century. Interestingly the group did not foray into Steel initially, the commodity it is famous for today. The founder of the Rathi Group, Seth Gordhan Das Ji Rathi, along with his brothers, began trading in cloth. They were based out of a small shop in Katra Asharfi in Chandni Chowk.

The brothers used to travel to Ahmedabad, Gujrat, to source fabric and would sell it in Delhi. As a result of their hard work, business acumen and ethical business practices, the business grew, and they prospered. Soon, somewhere in the 1900s, the brothers, under the leadership of Gordhan Das Ji, bought their own piece of real estate in the prime location of Nai Sadak, Chandni Chowk.

From operating out of a small rented shop in a Katra, the group went to building their own Katra, obviously named the Rathi Katra. It was a huge achievement indeed. It was a well-constructed six-story building, the best among its contemporaries. The bottom four floors housed the cloth market, while the top 2 floors were the residence of the entire Rathi family.

The business was booming, and this was evident in the fact that the Rathi family was among the few families that owned Horse carriages and Horses and was privileged to be able to offer employment to a huge domestic & security staff.

The family was working hard and living happily. Little did they know that life had other not-so-pleasant plans for them.

On a day like any other, on his return from one of his visits to Ahmedabad in the 1920s, Seth Gordhan Das ji Rathi came to know that the entire stock of cloth in their shop had been sold to one single trader. Gordhan Das Ji did not react positively to this news as he felt it was not a wise decision, and of course, he proved to be right.

This trader then declared himself bankrupt, causing a huge shocking loss of more than Rs. 10 lacs to the family in those times.

Due to this, the family suffered huge financial loss and as the wise say, desperate times call for desperate measures... Seth Gordhan Das ji Rathi rose to the occasion and demonstrated his wisdom and his character of steel. Despite having lived a life of luxury, he was a grounded man and made some radical decisions to lead his family through the financial crisis, like giving the Horse Carriage to the driver free of cost, removing all the guards, doing away with all the lights in the house except one in each room. He even took on the duty of locking all the doors, including the main door, upon himself. This was all done in order to cut costs.

After this professional disaster, when Seth Gordhan Das ji Rathi went to Ahmedabad to buy cloth, no mill owner was ready to give him material on credit. But Men of character and integrity are a different breed altogether. To everyone's surprise, Set Gordhan Das ji said- "I don't want material on credit. I have money to buy 1 bale of cloth, and I will buy only one bale".

Demonstrating exemplary courage and resilience, he eventually restarted the business again with that one bale of cloth. Due to his moral ethics and clean business practices, he was able to re-establish the business soon.

And it is this strength, integrity and honesty that are reflected in every product and business practice of the Shri Rathi Group even today. We carry forward the legacy of this respected leader in spirit and product.

The Man with a Character of Steel Finally Enters the Steel Industry

Always blessed with a keen sense of business, in 1942, Seth Gordhan Das ji saw a good business opportunity in the Copper Rolling business and decided to close down the existing cloth trading business and, along with his younger brother and nephew, established a Copper Rolling Mill by the name of RATHI BROTHERS at Loni Road, Shahdara.

The rolling mill proved to be a good decision. Business continued to grow by leaps and bounds and kept scaling up with every step.

- Around the end of WORLD WAR 2, a rolling mill to manufacture steel rounds and other items was set up.

- Then, in the early 1960s, a semi-automatic rolling mill was imported from Japan, the first of its kind in North India.

- In 1964, RATHI collaborated with TOR ISTEG STEEL CORPORATION of LUXEMBOURG through Tor Steel Research Foundation in India to manufacture TOR STEEL (well known as Saria in the market) in India. This helped reduce steel consumption by up to 40% in construction activities.

- It is our pride and honour to be the pioneers--- the first company in India to start the manufacturing of TOR STEEL in India.

- With this, India's most trusted & most famous brand of Saria... Rathi Saria, was born.

- Beginning with a humble production capacity of 369 kg daily, today, RATHI is North India's biggest brand selling more than 21 lac tons every year. This is many times more than even the combined sales of other brands.

- This has been possible because the market trusts Rathi as India's oldest and best brand due to the group's integrity, quality and ethics.

- In addition to this, in the past 80 years of its operations, the Rathi Group has pioneered many other firsts, such as-

  a. The Branding of Steel Products to certify authenticity. We were the first to start this practice

in 1966. Before that, there was no way of identifying a premium product from any regular product. Steel was just steel before this.

b. The Rathi Group was the first business group to give North India its first Steel Plant.

c. We were also the first to start using Natural Gas (PNG) in our plants.

Sharing with you a part of the growth of the legacy of the Rathi Group with some rare and precious pictures from the archives.

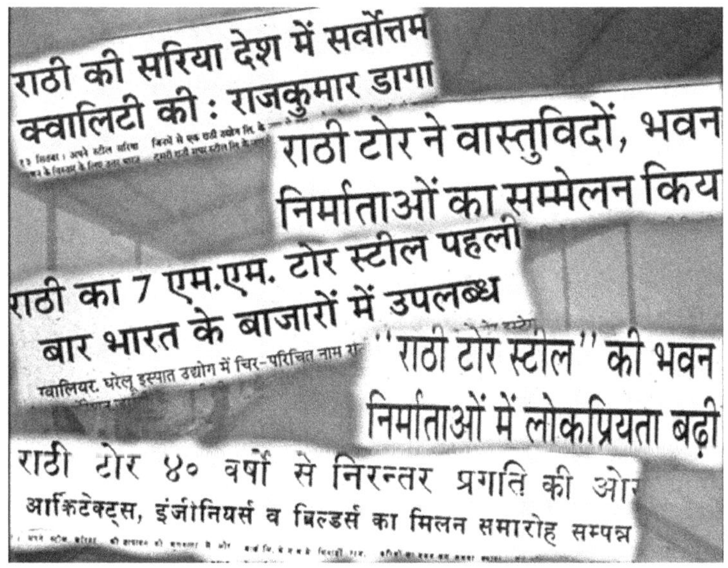

राठी की सरिया देश में सर्वोत्तम क्वालिटी की : राजकुमार डागा
राठी टोर ने वास्तुविदों, भवन निर्माताओं का सम्मेलन किय
राठी का 7 एम.एम. टोर स्टील पहली बार भारत के बाजारों में उपलब्ध
''राठी टोर स्टील'' की भवन निर्माताओं में लोकप्रियता बढ़ी
राठी टोर ४० वर्षों से निरन्तर प्रगति की ओर
आर्किटेक्ट्स, इंजीनियर्स व बिल्डर्स का मिलन समारोह सम्पन्न

Challenges Forge Us Stronger

However, as is the case with every business, the growth of the Rathi group was also not linear and smooth by any means. The group faced and overcame many challenges.

On the upside, RATHI STEEL was growing at a phenomenal rate. By 1972, the family had set up 6 plants spread across North India, with a major concentration in the state of Uttar Pradesh. RATHI was considered the leading brand in Steel in North India.

But, due to a 100% power cut in the state of Uttar Pradesh in the late 1970s, the majority of the family's plants were forced to close down. The situation continued for more than 7 years, leading to huge losses for the family and almost a total destruction of the business.

Fed up with the situation, in 1977, Sh. Prem Ratan Rathi, the eldest son of our founder Seth Gordhan Das ji Rathi, decided to do something about it and managed to persuade the Uttar Pradesh Government to give at least partial power to industries. Finally, the government agreed to give power to industries for a minimum of 8 hours a day.

With this partial relief (that happened only because of the steely determination of the RATHI Family), not only did our business start getting streamlined again, but more plants mushroomed across India along with the modernisation of existing plants.

In 1988, our plant at Loni Road, Shahdara, was considered to be one of the most efficient steel rolling mills in North India.

However, there were more challenges on the horizon (though they were negotiated peacefully and amicably); as the years passed, the RATHI Family expanded, and so did the business.

By 2003s, the family had split into 7 groups, each having its independent steel manufacturing units.

Carrying on the legacy of the 1st & Oldest Name in Steel

The Shri Rathi Steel Group was founded by our father, Mr Anil Rathi, the youngest son of Seth Gordhan Das ji Rathi, in the year 2002. We joined him in 2002 and 2003, respectively.

The group's first plant, M/s. Shri Rathi Steel Limited started production in the year 2003 in Ghaziabad with an installed capacity of 1,00,000 MT per Annum of High Strength Steel Bars.

Continuing his father's legacy, our Chairman, Mr Anil Rathi, established the Shri Rathi Group as a quality producer of high-strength steel bars.

Due to the high demand for the products of Shri Rathi Group, another steel plant in the name of M/s. Shri Rathi Steel Dakshin Limited was commissioned in the year 2007. This increased the total installed capacity of Shri Rathi Group to 2,00,000 MT per Annum.

The Core Management Team at Shri Rathi Group

Core Management Team at Shri Rathi Steel Group

Mr. Anil Rathi, CMD (Age 66yrs)

Mr. Anil Rathi has a career spanning about 48 years in the fields of production planning, procurement, finance, etc in the Iron and Steel Industry. He holds a degree in Commerce from Shri Ram College of Commerce, Delhi University. He monitors the day-to-day affairs of the Company. His expertise lies in the technical department.

Mr. Gopal Rathi, Director (Age 41yrs)

Mr. Gopal Rathi, holds degree in Business Studies from Lancaster University (UK) and has a career spanning almost 20 years in the Iron & Steel sector. He is highly recognized in the steel industry for his analytical capability and fair business dealings. He has been on our Board of Directors since incorporation of the Group.

Mr. Dhruv Rathi, Director (Age 40yrs)

Mr. Dhruv Rathi holds a Degree in Management and Information Technology from University of Manchester Institute of Science and Technology (UK) and has joined the Group as a whole time Director in the year 2003. His expertise lies in the field of incorporating technology within the existing systems to cut costs and increase outputs.

Mr. Anil Rathi, our chairman, is renowned in the industry for his transparent & ethical business practices. In fact, here is an interesting and surprising fact that not many people know about. Strength and quality are not limited to our product only, they are a huge part of his character like they were with his father and the founder of the Rathi Group. Dear readers, you will all be surprised and inspired to know that our chairman completed his B.com Degree from Delhi University in 2022 after appearing for his 3rd-year examination, which he had missed due to work pressure earlier.

In 2022 Delhi University declared that any student who had ever missed their 3rd-year exam could sit for them and complete their degree. Taking advantage of this and shattering all age-related myths, Mr Anil Rathi proudly graduated from the prestigious Shri Ram College of Commerce. This bears high testimony to his grit and determination.

It is due to his strength of character, futuristic vision and experienced approach that the SHRI RATHI GROUP is the most successful group in the entire RATHI Group with the maximum capacity and most number of plants.

After completing college in London, both of us brothers have matched our chairman (and father) stride for stride and, with his guidance and blessings, have scaled up the strategy, innovations and technology in the business to carry the trusted RATHI name and legacy forward. We are indeed blessed and humbled that the industry recognises our hard work and innovation by considering us experts in our domain, and we are regularly invited to address conferences, seminars and other Industry events.

Place the pictures of Mr Dhruv & Gopal Rathi speaking and being awarded in this section.

Acknowledging our dedication to quality and work ethics, the INDUSTRY OUTLOOK MAGAZINE recognised us as one of the TOP 10 TMT BAR MANUFACTURERS in 2023. We were the only manufacturer from North India to make that coveted list.

We are also India's first company to export TMT Bars to AMERICA. Delighted to share with you some pictures of the material being dispatched to NELLIS AIR FORCE BASE, the largest base on the West Coast of America.

Sharing with you some more info (facts and figures) about the Shri Rathi Group.

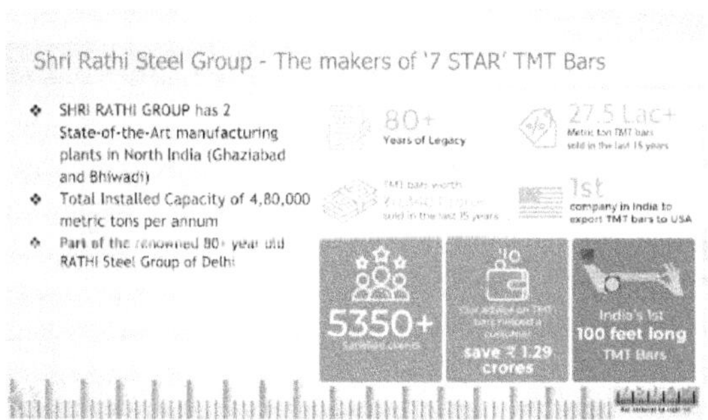

We have 2 plants, one in Ghaziabad, U.P & the other in Bhiwadi, Rajasthan. Both of these are among the most modern plants of North India.

Our monthly production capacity is 40,000 tons which is the maximum in this area; interestingly, we increased this capacity during the Covid pandemic.

As part of the famous RATHI GROUP in the last 15 years, we have sold 27.5 lacs ton of material (Saria) worth Rs.11,340 crores.

And to give you just one example out of the many, we saved a client ₹1.29 Crore by giving them the right advice. Little wonder then that we have more than 5350 satisfied clients across the globe.

The Incredible Growth Story of the Shri Rathi Group

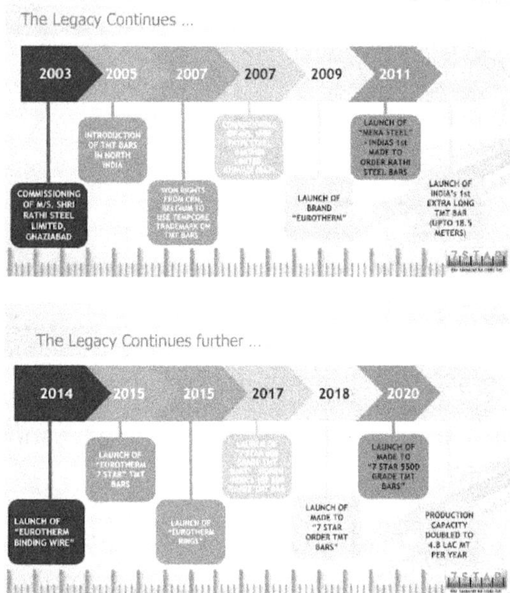

A Look at Our Product Portfolio

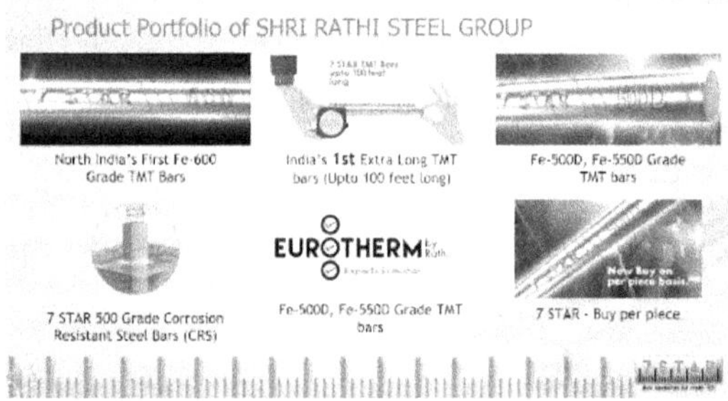

In total, we offer 7 types of Bars (Saria) in our portfolio; there is something suited to nearly every application:

- 7 STAR 600 Grade Steel Bar - North India's first 600 Grade Bar.

- India's first 100 Feet Long Bar- that can save you up to 29 % of material usage and thus cost.

- 500 Chemical, 500D Chemical, 550 Chemical, 550D Chemical.

- We are North India's only manufacturer of 500 Grade Corrosion Resistant Steel (CRS), especially developed by us for the CPWD.

- Our 7 STAR 500 D Bar, and we proudly sell it in 12 Mtr pieces; buy only what you need. No hassle of buying by weight.

Mr Dhruv being awarded for innovation in TMT Bars by the Indian Institute of Architecture, Rajasthan Chapter.

Our 7 STAR TMT Bar Stall at the Credai Youthcon event attended by our PM Shri Narendra Modi Ji. Here we displayed our new inovative products like the Extra Long Bar & the 600 Grade Bar.

Our 7 STAR TMT Bar Stall at Asia's leading trade fair for architecture, building materials, art and design, ACE TECH, DELHI

It is indeed a testimony to our quality, ethics, innovation and hard work to count these prestigious names among our clients.

We regularly supply material to private & government departments such as CPWD, IOCL Panipat Refinery, Barmer Refinery Project, NBCC, Bharat Petroleum, UP Awas Vikas, Rajasthan Housing Board, Up PWD

We are also an approved vendor for NHAI projects. Also, we are the official suppliers to all the AMITY University Campuses at Noida, Manesar, Jaipur, Lucknow and Gwalior.

Meet some of our industrial clients in the private sector like Haldiram, GMR (Delhi Airport), TATA Power, Rajnigandha, KENT RO, Cornitos, Liberty Shoes, Jai Bharat Maruti etc.

Not to forget our prestigious clients in Real Estate. These a e all the top real estate players of Delhi-NCR.

Certifications and Accreditations with the Shri Rathi Group.

These certifications and accreditations speak volumes about our quality and process.

- We have been granted a BIS License for every grade of the product.

- Our TMT manufacturing technology is approved by the TEMPCORE Group of Belgium. To give you an idea of our quality, please know that TEMPCORE is the same technology used by TATA STEEL & SAIL for manufacturing TMT. In fact, we are one of the very few TMT manufacturers in India who are permitted to write TEMPCORE on our Bars.

- We have gone another step further and acquired the technology for the calculations from HEEP & P of Germany.

- And, of course. We are ISO 9001, ISO 14001 & ISO 18001 certified.

The 4P Growth Framework for TMT Dealerships

Now that we have together revisited the glorious history and legacy of the Rathi Group and the birth of the Shri Rathi Group carrying forward this legacy grandly...

There is something of great importance that we want to share with you.

Whenever we are asked the question of what makes the Shri Rathi Group super successful- Apart from our quality, integrity and innovation, we have only one answer—

It is our Dealers that make us super successful!
They are the lifeline of the Shri Rathi Group!

And we are completely dedicated to the growth and success of our Dealers and strive hard to think up new ways to empower them even further- for we are FAMILY.

Our wins are interconnected; If they win, we win.

With this intent, in addition to arming them with top-quality, state-of-the-art products and offering them unbeatable commercials, we have worked hard to develop the 4P GROWTH FRAMEWORK that is guaranteed to give you 3X consistent growth in your TMT Dealership.

This book is written especially for you- our precious family of Dealers to help you achieve new benchmarks of success and grow your dealership by leaps and bounds in a smooth and speedy manner.

- If you are already a part of this family, with this book, you will be able to take your dealership to new heights.

- If you are a part of the TMT Bar industry and are not a part of the Shri Rathi family- it will show you what success and profitability you are missing out on by not being a part of this family so that you can join the family at the earliest and be a part of our roaring success.

- If you are an entrepreneur/aspiring entrepreneur looking for a great business opportunity, well then you are holding the right book in your hand as it will show you how being a part of the Shri Rathi Group family with a TMT Bar Dealership is the perfect business opportunity for sustained growth and success.

Ok, we understand that you are all eager to understand the 4P Growth Framework and get cracking to implement it and reap the benefits speedily, so without further ado, let's dive in deep:

What is the 4P Growth Framework?

Basically, this framework is your Formula for a Fast Growth Dealership

Change + Evolution + Speed = Consistent Growth

What this means is that to grow, you must accept that times, trends & technology are changing at a fast pace, and you need to embrace and keep up with these changes and evolve constantly.

This is where the 4P Growth Framework comes in- It will show you and firmly set you on the path to growth and success.

The four essential parts that make up the process of achieving Guaranteed 3x Consistent Growth in your TMT Dealership are referred to as the 4P Growth Framework. The 4 Ps of the Growth Framework are Profitability, Peace, Productivity and Preferred Partnership.

These fundamental parts sum up the Four P's definition. They include a holistic business strategy and a combination of techniques a TMT Dealership can use to get Guaranteed 3x Consistent Growth.

The effectiveness and efficiency of the 4P Growth Framework lie in its simplicity, practicality and ease of implementation.

We have condensed all our learning, knowledge, expertise, global exposure and experience into this 4P Growth Framework, and we are confident of the transformational results.

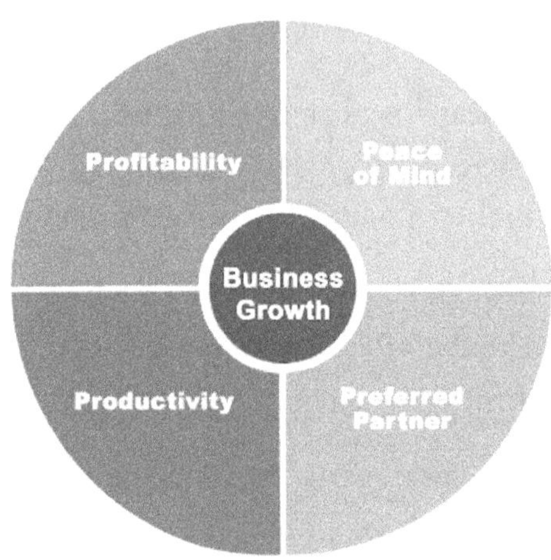

The Inspiration/Origin of the 4P Growth Framework

The original 4P Growth Framework has a long and illustrious history. Our 4P Growth Framework has been conceptualized on the science of the 4 Ps Marketing first proposed by Neil Borden, a professor at Harvard University in an article titled "The Concept of the Marketing Mix" in 1964.

The Importance of the 4 Ps of the 4P Growth Framework

Being a part of this industry for generations now, we understand the typical challenges the owner of a TMT Dealership encounters. Therefore, the Growth Strategy of this Framework revolves around the 4 Ps that a TMT Dealership Owner aspires for:

1. Increasing Profitability through increased market reach and repeat orders.

2. Peace of mind through additional profit, non-indulgence in unfair business practices and safeguarding market and money through an exclusive area.

3. Higher productivity of the business owner by making systems which help the owner of the TMT dealership to focus more on customers, increase wallet share with existing customers and ultimately help them make a USP for themself in the market.

4. Establish their dealership as a preferred partner and increase its perceived value in the eyes of the customer.

Let's understand the 4P Growth Framework in detail below:

1. **Profitability**

   a. Higher repeat orders with almost NIL involvement

   Steel bar dealers can achieve higher repeat orders with minimal involvement by consistently providing excellent products and services. Satisfied customers will naturally return for more, resulting in increased repeat business and reduced efforts to secure new orders.

   b. Taking advantage of the sales support of the manufacturer

   Secondary sale support from manufacturers can help steel bar dealers grow their businesses. It provides competitive pricing, product training, technical assistance, and marketing materials to attract more customers and boost sales. This is something that most dealers tend to overlook and do not take full advantage of.

c. Making a strong lead management and collection system

A lead management system is important for resellers as it helps organize and track potential customers, ensuring efficient follow-up and maximizing conversion rates. It enables resellers to prioritize leads, nurture relationships, and ultimately increase sales opportunities. Without a proper system in place, your leads are likely to get lost, and as a result, your follow-ups will be random & chaotic, leading to a much lower conversion rate than what is potentially possible.

d. Using Digital Marketing to increase leads

With the world going digital, it is important to work according to the changing business trends and leverage technology. Digital marketing is essential in today's time; it can boost lead generation by reaching a wider audience through various online channels like social media, email campaigns, and search engine optimization. It allows businesses to target specific demographics and engage potential customers, resulting in increased leads and potential sales.

e. **Indulge in influencer activities to create loyalty**

With the advent of social media, today, influencers have a lot of persuasive power and credibility in their niche. Engaging in influencer activities is important for creating loyalty. When businesses collaborate with influencers, they can reach a wider audience, build trust, and foster loyalty among their followers, resulting in increased customer retention and advocacy.

2. **Peace of Mind**

a. **Attracting a New Generation of Dealers & Leaders**

Most dealership owners are concerned about succession. They are unsure if the next generation will carry the business and legacy forward. These concerns can be addressed and overcome by creating a platform such that the new generation of dealers will join them willingly.

To attract the new generation, resellers should provide training, mentorship, and flexible work options. They should also promote the benefits and career opportunities available within their company to entice younger individuals to join their team.

b. **Transparent pricing policy resulting in loyal customers**

Having a transparent pricing policy can lead to loyal customers. When customers trust that the pricing is fair and transparent, they feel more confident in their purchasing decisions and are more likely to remain loyal to the business. This lessens many hassles associated with business, negotiations and discounts, leading to more peace of mind for the business owner.

c. Create trust and credibility amongst new and existing customers

Creating trust and credibility is essential for both new and existing customers. It helps businesses build strong relationships, retain customers, attract new ones, and ultimately grow their reputation and success. When you know that your customers and collaborators trust you implicitly and explicitly, that is a lot of weight off your shoulders.

d. Adopting Fair & Transparent business practices to increase business growth

Fair and transparent business practices are crucial for increasing business growth. By being honest, ethical, and treating customers and partners fairly, businesses build trust, loyalty, and a positive reputation, attracting more customers and fostering long-term success. And knowing that they have been fair to all and created a win-win for everyone, the business owner can sleep peacefully each night.

e. **Elimination of malpractices by dealers to make a profit**

Eliminating malpractices by dealers is crucial for making profits. It ensures fair competition, builds trust with customers, maintains a positive reputation, and avoids legal issues that can harm the business in the long run.

3. **Productivity**

a. **Faster customer conversion rate due to a higher level of trust and confidence**

Steel bar dealers can achieve a faster customer turnaround rate by building higher levels of trust and confidence. When customers trust the dealer's expertise and quality, they are more likely to make quick purchasing decisions, leading to increased sales and customer satisfaction.

b. **Increase in the wallet share of the customer using cross-selling techniques**

To increase the wallet share of customers, the best way is to use cross-selling techniques. By offering additional products or services that complement their purchase, customers are encouraged to spend more, resulting in higher revenue and customer satisfaction.

c. **Reduction in time spent on procurement of TMT bars**

Reducing the time spent on TMT bar procurement is crucial for business growth. It allows dealers to focus on other essential activities like sales and customer service, leading to increased productivity, faster order fulfilment, and improved customer satisfaction, which ultimately drives business growth.

d. Removal of price negotiations and objections by the customer

To eliminate price negotiations and objections from customers, a dealer can focus on clearly communicating the value of their products, offering competitive pricing, and providing transparent pricing information upfront. Building trust and showcasing the benefits of the products can also help minimize objections.

4. Preferred Partner

a. Creating an organized business platform resulting in a higher perceived image of the dealership.

Creating an organized business platform can enhance the dealership's perceived image. By maintaining efficient processes, clear communication, and a professional appearance, customers view the dealership as reliable, trustworthy, and competent, leading to a stronger and positive reputation.

b. Establishing themselves as a preferred reseller in the market

To establish themselves as a preferred reseller in the market, a dealer should focus on offering exceptional customer service, providing high-quality products, building strong relationships with customers, and consistently delivering value.

c. Getting preference from customers

To gain preference from customers, a dealer should prioritize customer satisfaction by providing excellent products, reliable service, and personalized experiences. Building strong relationships and consistently delivering value will help earn customer loyalty and preference.

d. Creating an environment of trust and genuineness in the eyes of the customer

Creating an environment of trust and genuineness is helpful for business growth as it fosters strong customer relationships, enhances loyalty, attracts new customers through positive word-of-mouth, and establishes a reputable brand image.

e. Choosing a brand offering a monopolistic market to the dealer and safeguarding their market.

In a monopolistic market, resellers can benefit from higher profit margins due to limited competition. Additionally, they can have increased financial security as monopolistic suppliers often provide stable prices and consistent product availability, reducing the risk of fluctuating costs or shortages.

Now that you understand the 4P Growth Framework and its components clearly, in the next section of the book, we will discuss 9 important Real-Life Situations which are critical for the growth of a TMT bar Dealership.

If these situations are not dealt with properly, the results can be catastrophic. They can even lead to the closure of decade-old TMT dealerships.

However, let us assure you that you are safe. All you need to do is kindly sit back and go through these situations and learn how to handle them very carefully, as you might also be facing one or many of them regularly.

Getting repeat orders from customers with NIL involvement

Mungeri Lal Ke Hassen Sapne Sach Hue: With 7 Star Dreams Became a Reality!

We met a dealer who had been selling TMT bars for the last 40 years in the same locality. We discussed what had changed in the business in the last 4 decades. He said the business was good and very profitable when he first started. He was the only TMT dealer of a particular brand in the area. He was able to charge a premium from customers. Repeat sales were high as he was the only dealer. Times were good, and he was able to expand into other categories, build a house, and send his children for higher education to the best universities in the country. He was known as *"the Saria wala"* in that area.

Then over a period of time, new dealerships started opening first 1, then the second and now **there are 8-10 dealers within a vicinity of a 3 km radius. All are selling the same brand. There is no USP with any dealer.** They are either selling on credit or at a very less margin. Some dealers are even using unethical ways to increase their margins as they can't increase prices due to the cutthroat competition. Now profitability had reduced considerably, and they were facing challenges in surviving even.

After listening to his problem, we asked him to visualize a scenario- ''Imagine you are back in time. You are once again the only dealer of a particular brand in your area and have no competition for selling that particular brand from other dealers. You can be assured that you will get the best price, and no one can undercut you. There is full customer support in terms of marketing and service from the company. You will never ever have to do anything unethical to earn profits. Customers will themselves give you a higher price. How does it feel?

He said it's like "Mungeri Lal ke haseen sapne"

His answer was interesting and rather hilarious, referencing a popular TV series where the protagonist dreams impossible dreams that never come true.

But we made this dream turn into reality when he became associated with 7 Star, where he was assured exclusivity within a radius of 3 km and best price policy. The company ensured that the dealer was provided with all the marketing collateral, and the dealer's sales staff were given proper training about the benefits of different grades and the quality of TMT bars which no other brand had ever done. The dealer's shop was redefined and made into a company shoppe displaying the company product and educational posters across the shop.

7 Star also had a USP of selling TMT by piece instead of weight on the basis of a weekly Recommended Consumer

Price (RCP). The customer was assured that he paid for what he was buying as counting is much easier than weighing, and it also eliminated the risk of theft in transit and at customers' sites.

I met the Dealer again after 6 months and asked him how's the business running now.

The dealer said he was extremely happy. It was as if his whole life had changed. He no longer had to run behind the customer.

His shop was attracting customers like a magnet. There were repeat customers on his terms and prices. He was super confident that no one could offer the 7 Star Brand in his area of exclusivity.

RCP increased the trust amongst the customer and profits in the balance sheet. It was a Win-Win situation for both.

As profitability was increasing day by day, he had reduced his debt by 25% in 6 months and was confident of being debt free in the next 1 year.

This is the magic of 4P Framework's "4th P" - Preferred Partner!!!

As opposed to the scenario in the above case, in the traditional scenario, even after convincing the customer to buy from them and giving a lower rate to start the relationship, the dealer is never sure that they will get the order because the customer will always hunt around for the lowest price without focusing on benefits and may even be cheated by some dealers indulging in unethical practices.

And even if the dealer gets the order, they can never be sure that they will get repeat orders from the customer. The dealer fears that whenever the customer will have the next requirement, they will follow the above-mentioned cycle before finalizing the order. In short, the dealer isn't sure of the repeat business even after selling at lower margins.

And even if we assume that the dealer is able to retain a customer.

1. Does the dealer have a mechanism to make the customer trust that the price being offered to them is correct? They may suspect that the dealer is looting them.

2. After some deliveries, if a customer is able to get a lower price for the same brand from another vendor, will they not feel cheated?

3. Will the customer not try to deduct the difference from the outstanding amount of the dealer, thinking he has looted him in past dealings?

4. Is there a possibility for the dealer to safeguard themself from this risk and, at the same time, keep the customer happy?

Yes, of course, like the dealer in the above real-life example, you can use the 4th 'P: Preferred Partner' of the 4P Growth Framework to overcome this situation.

1. Due to product monopoly, the dealer can be 100% sure that if the customer is satisfied with the product, they will surely come back with repeat orders.

2. Being a preferred dealer of the company, the dealer enjoys preferential booking, timely delivery and sales support from the company. This further strengthens the chances of getting repeat orders from the customer.

3. Customer will not be able to get a better price from anyone else as no one has that brand or no one can offer better rates than the dealer.

4. Dealers with a Monopoly area also have a higher level of trust in the eyes of the customer as to why only this dealer has been given exclusivity for this brand.

5. When the dealer is working with a trusted and reputed brand, they automatically create trust and credibility amongst new and existing customers.

6. When customers realize the dealer has an area exclusivity with the brand and no one else can offer them the same product, it helps increase the trust in the eyes of the customer.

7. Once a customer has full trust in the dealer, they are also willing to buy the other products the dealer has to offer. The dealer will benefit from upselling and cross-selling. e.g. they can also sell Cement, Tiles, Sanitaryware etc.

8. Once a customer develops trust, they will not negotiate again and again with the dealer. they will just convey their requirement and take delivery. The dealer will be free from the annoying daily bargaining on price. ***Roz roz ki price ki chik chik hi khatam ho jayegi.***

Wasting precious time in the purchase of TMT bars rather than in Sales

Focus on Priorities: Time is Money

During our recent Holi Milan, we met one of our dealers from UP. During the discussion, he told me how he was able to increase his sales by 70% by doing just one thing.

That one thing was so logical and simple, but still, he was not doing it for the last so many years. He has been a dealer of TMT bars for the last 5 years, but he was spending all his time at the shop trying to find the cheapest price of the brand of TMT he was selling. As the brand he was selling had a great pull demand, his zero effort in sales was not affecting his growth.

But as competition increased and many new dealerships selling the same brand opened in his area, he started facing sales issues, and thus, he started giving more discounts to retain his customers.

Hence, he started spending even more time trying to find a source from which he could buy the same TMT brand at a lower price. The whole day, he was just calling different distributors of the same brand to get the lowest price. But the situation was getting worse every day because perhaps all other dealers of the same brand in his area were also doing the same.

One fine day, he got an offer to become an exclusive dealer for a NEW BRAND which didn't change the price every 2 hours but had a single price for 1 week and printed "Recommended Consumer Price" (RCP) valid for 1 week.

The company made sure that the dealer didn't have to bear the loss of market fluctuation and gave a rate guarantee up to 3 days from dispatch, i.e. if there is any rate change within 3 days of dispatch from the factory to the dealer's shop, the dealer will get a credit note for the rate difference, thus, protecting the dealers from any rate fluctuation as dealers are generally able to turn around their stock within 3 days. Now he wasn't worried about buying at the lowest price.

Now that he was free from daily chik chik of rates, he started to focus on his marketing strategy and other marketing-related activities to boost sales as he didn't have to spend a single minute purchasing as rates were fixed.

With time in hand, he established a simple yet effective lead management system, started following up with his old clients, the TMT company made his shop into a showroom so that it looks nice & organized and also started some influencer marketing.

He continued these activities for almost 5-6 weeks, and gradually, he started getting customers who were ready to buy at this price and terms. His profitability increased, repeat sales started, and his credit reduced in the market.

Today, his shop is the highest-selling TMT shop in the whole area.

This is the magic of 4P Framework's "3rd P" - Productivity!!!

Now let's look at the traditional scenario instead of the example shared above.

The dealer is wasting a lot of time and energy in trying to ascertain the best purchase price in the market rather than spending time and energy on selling. Even after making the buying decision at the best price available to them, they continue to be dissatisfied as they aren't sure if they got the best rates or not.

For example

1. Suppose in the morning at 11 am, the companies open rates of TMT, and the trade is 50000 per MT for a particular brand.

2. After continuously discussing with 15 traders and 4 companies till 4 pm, the dealer finally gets the best price of 49600 PMT and books his order with the trader/company that is offering him the lowest price for the same brand.

3. He is still insecure, as mann hi mann (in his mind) he feels, had he spoken to 2-3 more traders he might

have got a better price, i.e. 49300. Even after trying hard and negotiating with 19 different sale points, he isn't happy as he is not confident of getting the best price.

4. This happens day after day, deal after deal!!!

5. Imagine so much time wasted in the wrong activity with insignificant results and add to it the dissatisfaction. All this could have been used to develop new marketing strategies, build a better lead management system, or set up better processes.

Here, the dealer should use the 3rd 'P: Productivity' of the 4P Growth Framework to overcome this situation as demonstrated by the real-life example shared above.

1. Reducing the time spent on TMT bar procurement is crucial for business growth. It allows dealers to focus on other essential activities like sales and customer service, leading to increased productivity, faster order fulfilment, and improved customer satisfaction, which ultimately drives business growth.

2. Instead of trying to spend time on getting new customers, educating them and also making a lead management system, the dealer is only spending his time trying to assess the market, get an idea of the lowest price in the market, and ultimately take the decision. This time spent can even be up to 1-2 hours at times.

A Non-Monopolistic Market

Exclusive Monopoly: The Path to Progress

One of our dealers in Delhi has shown excellent performance in selling our premium brand, 7 STAR. He has been dealing in the RATHI brand since the 1980s and is a very famous and popular counter in his area. He started dealing in 7 STAR in October last year and is selling around 600-700 MT per month today. He sells 7 STAR only by piece and is earning a huge profit on each sale.

Recently, he requested us to meet a big real estate client, having a demand of 7000 MT of TMT bars for their project in Noida. While on our way back from the meeting, we asked him about his journey of selling 7 STAR and how he has been able to increase his sales in such a short period.

He told me that the main reason behind his success is 'MONOPOLY'. As 7 STAR is given to dealers on an exclusive basis in an area spread across 3 km, he was fully confident of the fact that his sales and promotional efforts for 7 STAR in his area and his regular clients couldn't be utilized by any other dealer as he has a Monopoly on 7 STAR in his area.

Secondly, he is also confident and at peace while pitching 7 STAR as he's fully aware that being an exclusive counter, he gets special pricing and sales support from the company. In fact, **each month, leads received from Digital marketing amounting to 100-150 MT are given to him by our company.**

Looking at his amazing performance, we have decided to give him preferential dispatches and additional sales support and also increased his quota of bookings during an upward market movement. It is only due to his commitment towards our brand that we, the directors of the company, are also accompanying him to meet his clients, as and when he requests.

This is the magic of 4P Framework's "4ᵗʰ P" – Preferred Partner!!!

Today, the market of TMT bars is very competitive, with a large number of shops located in major consumption areas.

Many popular brands don't follow a policy of offering exclusive areas to their dealers, and hence the same brand is available with many dealers in the area.

This results in price competition amongst the dealers.

1. Let's take the example of, say, a market, Khanpur in Delhi, where there are 4 shops right next to each other.

2. The same brand is available at all the 4 shops.

3. Whenever a customer comes to buy that brand, he visits all the shops as they are opposite/nearby to each other.

4. As all are selling the same brand, he will try to negotiate with all of them to get the best price.

5. There might also be times when a customer lies to the dealer about the price being offered to him by the other dealer.

6. But as the same brand is available with all the dealers and the dealer isn't confident whether his purchase price is the same or better than his competitors, he will match it thinking that the other dealer might have offered the customer a lower price.

However, as shown in the real-life example shared above, the dealer can use the 4th 'P: Preferred Partner' of the 4P Growth Framework to overcome this situation.

1. Choosing a brand which gives Monopoly for an area will always help you in protecting the customer made by you, ensure healthy margins and also safeguard your money.

2. You can also be at peace that a customer whom you convinced after making much effort will come back to you only.

3. The manufacturer also gives preference to a dealer having a Monopoly for an area like sales support, sharing of leads, preferential booking during rate increase etc.

4. So go ahead and make the choice to enjoy the benefits of being exclusive.

Is your new generation interested in joining your TMT dealership business?

Adapt to New Organized Ways of Working-Attract Gen Next to the Business like a Magnet

During a recent workshop attended by us on succession planning, I learnt about how the millennials, i.e., the generation born in the year 2000 and after, think and look at business. Due to their exposure and access to technology, they are used to a very organized system of working. If we tell them to work in the manner in which we have been working since we started the business, they will totally refuse. This is the main reason why the new generation is either not interested in joining their generation's old businesses or, even if they join, they hardly put in any effort in it.

On discussing this with one of our very old dealers over a cup of coffee, we realized that most of our 2nd or 3rd generation dealers are also facing similar problems. Although they are still selling TMT bars worth crores in a month, their level of happiness is constantly reducing.

The main reason behind this is that their new generation is not ready to join their dealership. They feel that their fathers' business is not that **'Organized' and 'Systematic' and it's not 'their cup of tea** to work the way their fathers have been doing'. **They also feel that with the increase in data mapping and transparency in business practices, the way in which they operate at present will have to be changed very soon.**

According to them, there is no scope for scaling up the business, i.e., opening new counters in different parts of the city or different cities altogether, as their physical presence at the shop is a must and **this a huge limitation to successful expansion or scaling up.**

Another major reason which comes to my mind is that the existing counter of TMT bars is very raw and does not provide a working environment which the young generation is used to or wants. Nowadays, we all want to go to shops that provide a premium shopping experience rather than those which don't. Shopping malls are a classic example of this. **Footfalls in shopping malls are increasing day by day, whereas footfall in shops of the same brand in a traditional market is reducing day by day.**

Hence, we strongly believe that if a TMT bar dealer is able to provide an organized and systematic working environment to his new generation, there's no reason why they will not join him. They are fully aware of the potential of the business, enjoy solid goodwill in the market, have legacy customers and also have a guiding force having tons of experience. **But the key thing here is 'giving that working environment and an organized work culture'.**

This is the magic of 4P Framework's "2nd P" – PEACE of Mind!!!

India has changed a lot over the years. Information Technology and the introduction of new-age business technologies like E-Commerce, Information exchange platforms, Internet banking etc., are making the new generation more comfortable with an organized and hassle-free way of doing business. But unfortunately, most TMT dealerships are still working the old-fashioned way and haven't upgraded their work culture and environment with time.

This will, sooner or later, pose a very big challenge for the TMT dealership owners to convince their new generation to join their dealership, as the new generation wants an organized and systematic work environment.

Apart from this, due to the current market scenario, a TMT bar dealership is often forced to use unfair and illegal means to make a profit in the business. This further poses a problem for the new generation to join the TMT Dealership.

Tell us honestly, when the next generation sees you practicing business unethically (which you are forced to do due to the market scenario- though we are offering you a way out), how would it impact them? Would they be motivated to join you in this new age where the new generation is so focused on ethical and sustainable practices?

Or, in fact, would you truly want them to enter the world of unfair practices?

Here, as a dealer, you should use the 2nd 'P: Peace of Mind' of the 4P Growth Framework to overcome this situation as-

1. Having a TMT dealership that ensures smooth working and regular inflow of required profit through ethical and legitimate means is the only way to encourage the next generation to join your business.

2. A feeling of being a preferred dealer of the company and enjoying the goodwill of doing business in a fair and transparent manner will make a perfect platform for the next generation

3. Having multiple USPs in the product and services being offered by you will also help in creating an ecosystem of repeated, satisfied and loyal customers. This will result in a lower rate ki chik chik, which is what the new generation approves of.

4. Most importantly, by doing business transparently and through effective SOPs, your TMT dealership can be scalable, and you will be able to open multiple outlets without being limited by the physical presence of the owner.

5. So, go ahead, and evolve with the changing times & trends, embrace the necessary change and become a magnet to the next generation that they see your business as the best fit with their career goals.

Sales Support from the brand

Going the Extra Mile to Offer Support

A couple of years ago, we happened to meet a dealer who was not a part of the Shri Rathi Group family, and we got generally talking about business. As we interacted, we learned that he was struggling with less profitability. On discussing further, we understood that he wasn't getting the right secondary sales support and guidance from the brand he was carrying. As we explained to him about our way of working and strongly supporting our dealership family, he expressed his desire to be a part of our family, and of course, after the necessary formalities, we welcomed him into the family.

While trying to understand his struggles with profitability, we understood that if we could increase the inflow of customers at his shop, that could do wonders for him, but there were many dealers in his locality, and the challenge was deep. Applying the 4P Framework, we asked him to participate in a few events along with us as sponsors, and we also supported him in many aspects, such as product and sales training.

This worked wonders; soon, people began referring him to customers saying, *"**Arre Dinesh ji sariya walae se le lo,**"* *achche admi hain"* (Buy from Dinesh Ji, the TMT Bar expert, he is a good person).

His perception totally changed in his market due to the events. People began viewing him as the go-to man for buying TMT Bars- needless to say that his struggles with profitability came to an end very soon.

This is the magic of 4P Framework's "1ˢᵗ P" – Profitability!!!

1. It is very important as a dealer for you to review whether the company you represent is supporting you fully in enhancing sales and marketing.

2. In these times of social media, everything is being sold online. Selling online is not an easy task for the dealer. Online sales needs a complete paraphernalia such as:

   a. Website,

   b. Landing page,

   c. SEO,

   d. Lead tracking,

   e. Tele callers to qualify the leads,

   f. Sales staff to speak to the leads and convince them to buy their brand,

   g. Regular follow-ups with the leads and

   h. Execution of the order.

3. Even if he desires to do so, the dealer doesn't have the time and skills to do it.

4. And if the dealer hires a digital marketing company to do all this, he is spending money without knowing if it will get him any leads or not.

Here the dealer can use the 1st 'P: Profitability' of the 4P Growth Framework to overcome this situation as shown in the real-life example shared above.

1. Secondary sale support from manufacturers can help steel bar dealers grow their businesses. It provides competitive pricing, product training, technical assistance, and marketing materials to attract more customers and boost sales.

2. In today's era of digital marketing through social media platforms, WhatsApp marketing and websites, the number of people searching for TMT bars is increasing daily. Connecting with potential buyers in your area is the key to increasing business. Here it all depends on the company support you get.

3. Engaging in influencer activities is important for creating loyalty. When businesses collaborate with influencers, they can reach a wider audience, build trust, increase loyalty and ultimately result in increased repeat business from the customer. If your company is focusing on supporting you with all these activities, it is easier for you to benefit from them.

No USP of the Dealer

At our Dealers Meets, we make it a practice to interact with our dealers and review their business personally. During one such meet, while interacting with a Delhi-based dealer, we learned that his TMT business is going down every day. He was finding himself unable to compete in price with a nearby dealer. The situation had become so bad that his years-old customers were also getting diverted. He tried to convince his customers, but because of higher prices, he was unable to compete and get the business.

We especially sent a senior person to his shop and also did a very detailed study of what his competitor was doing.

It came out that his competitor was manipulating the weight of the bundle. He was buying the same product from a company which was making a low-weight bundle and selling it to customers at higher weight by manipulating his weighing scale. As the customers didn't have any mechanism to check the weight of the bundle during receipt, he was able to make a profit by cheating them.

We immediately advised our dealer to start selling to his customers in pieces of exactly 12 meters and not by weight.

For the customer, it is easier to count the TMT bars as compared to weighing. He also educated the customers about how the other dealer was manipulating and cheating them.

Our dealer even removed the weight scale from his shop. This further increased the confidence of his customers.

He made selling by piece his USP.

After a month of hard work and educating the customers, he was able to get back all his old customers, as he was able to successfully overcome one of the key pain points of his customers i.e., 'getting exactly what they are paying for.'

This is the magic of 4P Framework's "4th P" – Preferred Partner!!!

Traditionally, since a dealer doesn't have any USP or best-assured price from the company, he either increases his credit period to the customer or reduces his margin and uses it as his USP to keep his regular customers as he is continually living in fear that the customer will get a better price elsewhere and will buy from there.

Apart from this, he isn't sure if he is able to offer the best price as he isn't confident of his purchase price - He has no option but to use unfair means to earn profit like weight manipulation on the scale, selling an underweight product, billing in fraudulent names, GST manipulation etc.

Yeh saab kaam koi bhi apni icha se nahi karta - Admni kharab nahi hota haalat kharab hote hain hain.

No person is wrong; it is the circumstances that force their hand.

- The fallout of these unethical practices is that the person doing it loses respect for their own self, and it also affects your goodwill and reputation in the market in the long run.

- Also, the persons begin to doubt and question their profession, wondering whether it is profitable at all without these manipulations and unethical practices. These doubts cause them to work less than their full capacity.

As a dealer in such situations, you should use the 4th 'P: Preferred Partner' of the 4P Growth Framework to overcome this situation.

1. In order to attract customers, the dealer should have a USP in terms of product offering or price offering to its customer.

2. If you are also selling and providing the same product, which is easily and widely available, the customer will come to you always asking for rate negotiation or credit facility.

3. Once such, USP can be providing TMT bars by piece and not by weight. This will help you in creating trust and reliability in the eyes of the customer, as the customer can be 100% sure that he's getting what he is paying for. In short, he will be sure that there's no theft in transit or manipulation of weight by you.

4. Another USP can be providing rate transparency to the customer and helping him save the time spent on negotiations before every order. The pricing mechanism should be such that the customer is 100% sure that he's getting the best price every time.

5. Creating awareness amongst customers or influencers through educational programs, occasional visits by the sales staff of your principal, and benefiting them through innovative product offerings are also seen as a USP of the dealer. These will help in creating customer loyalty and repeat business opportunities.

Dealer ki kamai ya to galat kaam karke aati hai ya -Tezi-Mandi se

Business Hai Satte Bazari Nahin:
"This is Business not Betting!"

During one of our interactions with one of the biggest TMT dealers in Gurgaon, I asked him why he looked so tense and depressed. What he said totally shocked us out of our wits.

He said he had incurred a loss of 25 lacs in the last 1 month in his dealership.

We knew his monthly sales were 1000 mt per month, totaling to 12000 mt per year. The general profit margin for dealers per ton is Rs 500. At the given profit rate, he should be earning 60 lacs a year. He has lost almost half of his yearly profit.

We asked him how it happened? After some digging, he confided in us and said he used to sell at a margin of 200 per ton to the customers instead of the 500 in order to retain them, which worked out to 24 lacs a year, which was actually a loss as his fixed cost and working capital cost were more than this.

So, in order to increase his profit, he started doing *tezi-mandi,* satta- meaning he tried to time the market by buying at lower rates and selling at higher rates to earn profits. Returns were indeed high when the rates of TMT increased, and he earned a bumper profit on his stock.

This worked well for 3-4 times and he earned 7.5 lacs extra in 4 transactions combined but then the disaster struck. When he purchased more than his required quantity, thinking that the rates would increase, Instead, the market nose-dived due to change in government policies and overnight he lost 25 lacs. His profit for the whole year.

We explained to him that if had the capability to time the market, then we would be God. One can never buy at the bottom and sell at the highest rates.

We are doing business and not SATTA BAZAARI (Betting).

It's a law of nature that the price decreases more than it increases.

We explained to him that while it may look lucrative, trying to increase profits by doing tezi-mandi and not focusing on increasing his profit margin on sales was the biggest mistake a dealer could make.

Be associated with a brand that promises you profit and peace of mind. Profits will come from Exclusivity, Area Monopoly, Best Price Guarantee, Marketing and Sales support by the company, etc.

All these activities will increase your profits and you will sleep in peace.

This is the magic of 4P Framework's "2nd P" – Peace of Mind!!!

1. As TMT is a commodity, business prices fluctuate many times a day, and a dealer who adoes not understand and use the power of the 4P Framework will try to buy more quantity at the price he feels is the best price. He tries to time the market, which in truth, is impossible. There are more instances where market prices behave totally in the opposite manner than the dealer thinks they will, resulting in major losses.

2. Business should be such that you are able to earn comfortably without the risk of tezi-mandi.

3. True joy and prosperity are when you are assured that X amount of sales will amount to X amount of profits and you feel confident & motivated to reach & exceed that number. ***Mazza to tab hai jab aap ko pata hai aap ko har MT bechne pe "x" amount ki kamai hogi.*** There is no risk of any loss.

The dealer should use the 2nd 'P: Peace' of the 4P Growth Framework to overcome this situation when:

1. Due to tough market conditions and a non-monopolistic market, the dealer is not able to make a justified return on his investment by normal means.

2. This forces him to resort to satte baazi like postponing his buying decision to the last minute in case he comes to know that the MANDI (Market) is going down. But he doesn't realize that, at times, he has sold more material than he has in his shop and then gets tensed about its purchase.

3. In such a situation, at times, he even loses money due to the high fluctuation in the rates on a daily basis.

4. It is important to understand that there is a compounding effect on profit in the business i.e. making regular profits helps in increasing the overall kitty. If the business is profitable on every transaction, then the impact of compounding will be so huge that the next generation of dealers will not have to look for a new avenue for work due to less or no profits in the current business.

5. This also ensures that all goals like education, the marriage of children, and planning his retirement are met without any uncertainty

6. As the product being sold by the dealer is easily and widely available, the price of the product is not in his hand.

7. He is also not sure if the customer can get cheaper rates than him for the same brand, as he doesn't have a monopoly in the area.

8. In some cases, some brands are available with almost all the dealers in the market, and thus, the competition is very intense. This forces dealers to indulge in unfair business practices and manipulations, as that becomes the only way to make money.

9. This fear, along with manipulations, results in a market condition where no dealer can make money through legitimate business practices.

10. Hence, all such dealers are doing things which are not legal without understanding the negative consequences of the same.

11. Choose to be associated with a principal who can support you, and help you define a USP instead of getting into a price war so that your profit margins are healthy on each transaction and you sleep easy knowing that you are a business owner and not a Sattebaaz!

Should the Dealer sell material manufactured in Company-owned plants or by Franchisees or by Contract Manufacturers?

Once Cheated- Always Careful- Trust only Company-Owned Plants

We recently met one of our very old distributors, and he shared the following experience:

"I recently supplied material of a brand which was being made by a franchise unit to a client in Greater Noida. The client was a retired army major, and he was using this material to make his house. When he got the material checked, the material was not as per BIS standards. When he inquired about that particular brand from the market, he was told that this brand only makes substandard material. He then came to my office and questioned my ethics of dealing with such a brand when it is known for making substandard material. He also called me a cheat!

Ever since, I deal only with brands being manufactured in Company-Owned plants. At least, there is a comfort that as they are making for their own brand, they are careful of the quality and also stand guarantee for it."

This is the magic of 4P Framework's "2nd P" – PEACE of Mind!!!

Nowadays, in many companies, at times, the same brand is being made by company-owned plants, by franchises or contract manufacturers, but the material is being sold in the same market at different rates.

Some dealers of the brand deal in the material which is being made in company-owned plants, some dealers deal in the material manufactured by franchises and some deal in the material manufactured by contract manufacturers.

During our meetings with numerous dealers in the last 6 months, we have heard-

1. Many times, franchise units are not at all concerned about the quality of the product and are making underweight or inferior quality products. As they are selling the material on their own terms and paying a royalty to the brand owner, such units are only concerned about their current profits and not about the future of the brand they are making.

2. These people only make material for that brand till the commercials suit them; once it doesn't work for them, they stop. Or if another brand offers them a better deal, they shift without any delay.

Yeh log sirf tab tak uss brand ke liye maal banate hain jab tak unhe padta aata hai. Jahan padta bandh ya fir kissi aur brand ne achi deal offer kar di yeh unke naam se banana chalu kar dete hain.

3. Underweight material does improve the margin of retailers, but it's life-threatening for the customer.

4. Architects/Structural Engineers design the house or building as per IS Norms, and if the material used is inferior, it will weaken the structure of the house. Chances are it might collapse, causing damage to the life and property of the customer. Most people make their house only once in a lifetime. Imagine if the customer loss, life,limb or property using compromised material due to the retailer's greed that he isn't able to earn from fair means and use unfair means – What a huge crime this is! *Yeh kitni galat baat hai !!!*

5. *Woh 1-2% kamane ke liye logon ki jaan se khelne ko tayar ho gaya -* That anyone would be willing to play with people's lives for a mere 1- 2% of profits --- SHOCKING !!!

6. The dealer's goodwill and reputation get affected in case the quality of the product he deals in is substandard and fails at the site. Afterall the dealer is the first point of contact for the customer. He is also the first person to hear and face customer grievances.

The dealer should use the 2nd 'P: Peace' of the 4P Growth Framework to overcome this situation.

1. Should deal with only company-owned Brands.

2. Alternatively, should work with companies who have 100% control over the quality of the contract manufacturers as they have their QC team doing production audits in the plant like TATA Steel.

3. You will also be at peace while dealing with a company which is quality conscious, as you will be sure that the company will stand guarantee for its product and not supply you with substandard material.

4. It is important to note that the dealer is the main point of contact for the customer and will also be the first person to hear and face customer grievances, in case of any quality issue.

Faster Complaint Resolution

We recently had a conversation with one of our distributors who works with big real estate clients and corporate clients. He told us that **he is ready and happy to give our company a premium of Rs. 300-400 pmt over other manufacturers only because of our system of standing guarantee for our quality and our fast complaint resolution system.**

He has been working with our brand for the last 20 years, but **for the last 10 years, he has been dealing with only us in the consumer segment.**

He believes that an efficient and fast complaint resolution mechanism of a company is very important for gaining the confidence of its clients.

TMT bars can also have defects like other products, but what is important is the way in which the complaint is addressed by the company. There are some companies which don't bother about quality complaints and keep prolonging their resolution, like visits etc, till the time the material is either consumed by the client or the material is sent back by the client and the brand is blacklisted.

He was sharing how his lacs of rupees were stuck with these big real estate and corporate clients for the last many years on account of quality issues in the material dispatched by him in the past. As no importance was given to such complaints by the TMT bar manufacturer he was dealing with earlier, he had to face all the financial consequences.

He had already paid the manufacturer the money in advance but got his money from his client after deduction on account of quality issues.

Of course, there are times when there are quality issues in the TMT bars, or the end customer has a problem which needs attention.

But there are some companies who are not bothered to resolve whenever there is a quality issue, resulting in-

- Negative marketing amongst the architects, builders and end users.

- Would anyone want to use a branded product where your complaints go unheard & unattended? *Kya koi bhi aisa branded product use karna chahega jiski quality complaint ki koi sunwai nahi hai ?*

- As a result, they will stop using that brand and will divert to the brand that addresses and resolves their complaint—*jahan problems ki sunwai ho. Complaints ki sunwai zyadatar un brands mein hoti hai jo company owned, company manufactured hoti hai.* It is mostly company-owned & company-manufactured brands that address & resolve complaints speedily.

- The company that sells products under its own brand will always be conscious and concerned about the quality and problems faced by its customers at all levels as they understand that it can earn a premium only and only when customers ask for their product - there has to be a pull demand and not push demand. They strongly believe that their future depends upon their present.

Here, the dealer should use the 2nd 'P: Peace' of the 4P Growth Framework to overcome this situation.

1. The company with whom you are dealing should stand guarantee for all its product, no matter which grades you buy

2. The quality controller of the company should speak to the customer who has made the complaint within 2 hours of receipt of the complaint.

3. In case the customer demands a visit, the quality controller should visit the customer within 48 hours of registering the complaint.

4. During the visit, the quality controller should try to convince the customer and resolve the complaint.

5. In case it's not resolved, the material should be replaced free of cost.

A Quick Recap
Before Your New Journey

By now, we are sure that you have a detailed understanding of the 4P Growth Framework and how it can be applied in the most common Real-Life Situations threatening/haunting TMT bar dealerships.

However, here's a quick recap of the framework in a nutshell that you can refer to any time that you are faced with a challenge that stops you from growing.

1. **Profitability**

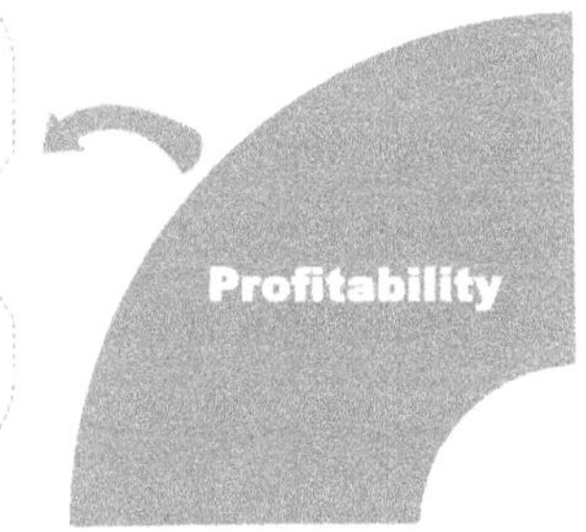

    a. Higher repeat orders with almost NIL involvement

    b. Taking advantage of the sales support of the manufacturer

    c. Making a strong lead management and collection system

d. Using Digital Marketing to increase leads

e. Indulge in influencer activities to create loyalty

2. **Peace of Mind**

a. Attracting a New Generation of Dealers & Leaders

b. Transparent pricing policy resulting in loyal customers

c. Create trust and credibility amongst new and existing customers

d. Adopting Fair & Transparent business practices to increase business growth

e. Elimination of malpractices by dealers to make a profit

3. Productivity

a. Faster customer conversion rate due to a higher level of trust and confidence

b. Increase in the wallet share of the customer using cross-selling techniques

c. Reduction in time spent on procurement of TMT bars

d. Removal of price negotiations and objections by the customer

4. Preferred Partner

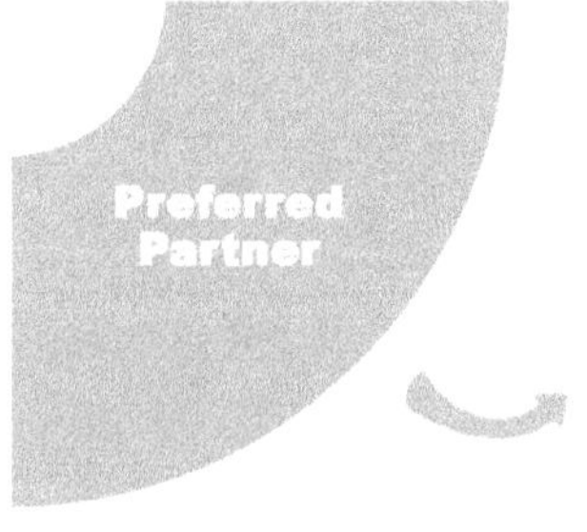

a. Creating an organized business platform resulting in a higher perceived image of the dealership

b. Establishing themselves as a preferred reseller in the market

c. Getting preference from customers

d. Creating an environment of trust and genuineness in the eyes of the customer

e. Choosing a brand offering a monopolistic market to the dealer and safeguarding their market

Each of these pillars of the Framework & their components has already been discussed in detail, along with their application to overcome real problems that you face every day and be free from them forever.

The Way Forward

We have seen the effects of the strategies of this framework in our business too. They are extraordinary if applied in the correct manner and with the correct spirit under the correct guidance.

Hence, we openly invite any of you who wants to understand in detail about the

4P Growth Framework and it's Guaranteed Science for 3x Consistent Growth in TMT Dealership.

Pl scan the QR code given below and fill out the Google Form. We will contact you shortly.

Also, we have created a **GROWTH MAP FOR YOUR TMT DEALERSHIP** based on the 4P Growth Framework.

And as a reward for being a serious action taker for the growth of your TMT Dealership, **this will be sent to the registered mobile number of the person who fills in the following QR Code.**

In our meeting, we will give you some more amazing yet simple tools, which can be applied in your business from day 1, no questions asked.

Together, we will create a growth plan for your TMT dealership like never done before. It will be a magical and transformational journey for you.

NOTES:

www.ingramcontent.com/pod-product-compliance
Lightning Source LLC
LaVergne TN
LVHW011304210726
843509LV00016B/779